Famous Illustrated
Speeches & Documents

THE STAR-SPANGLED BANNER

Stuart A. Kallen

Illustrations by Tim Blough

Published by Abdo & Daughters, 4940 Viking Drive, Suite 622, Edina, Minnesota 55435.

Library bound edition distributed by Rockbottom Books, Pentagon Tower, P.O. Box 36036, Minneapolis, Minnesota 55435.

Printed in the United States.

Interior Photo credits: Bettmann

Edited by Julie Berg

Library of Congress Cataloging-in-Publication Data

Kallen, Stuart A., 1955-
      The star-spangled banner / by Stuart A. Kallen.
            p.   cm. -- (Famous illustrated speeches)
      Includes index.
      ISBN 1-56239-317-0
      1. Key, Francis Scott, 1779–1843. Star-spangled banner--Juvenile literature.
      2. United States--History--War of 1812--Literature and the war--Juvenile
      literature.   3. Poets, American--19th century--Biography--Juvenile literature.
      4. Star-spangled banner (Song)--Juvenile literature.   [1. Star-spangled banner
      (Song) 2. United States--History--War of 1812.   3. Key, Francis Scott,
      1779–1843.]
      I. Title.   II. Series.
      PS2167.S73K35   1994
      811'.2--dc20
                                                                           94-12222
                                                                           CIP
                                                                           AC

INTRODUCTION

Imagine that you are living in the year 1814. Your country, the United States, is at war with Great Britain. Strange events have left you a prisoner on a British warship. All night long you watch in horror as the ship's cannons pound the fort that is defending your city.

Through hours of battle and clouds of cannon smoke, you see the flag of the United States flying above the fort. You are afraid when the flag disappears in the darkness of night. At dawn, you see the flag is still there. You scribble a quick poem on the back of an envelope that sums up your feelings. Later in the day, you are released by the enemy. You go home and finish your poem, put it to music, and have it printed. Years later, your song is sung by millions and millions of people.

It might be hard to imagine today, but that really happened to a man named Francis Scott Key. The War of 1812 was raging when Key wrote his song, the "Star-Spangled Banner." That song would later become the national anthem of the United States of America. This is the story of that song.

The War of 1812 was fought between the United States and Great Britain. It lasted from 1812 to 1815. On August 24, 1814, three weeks before Key wrote the "Star-Spangled Banner", British troops invaded Washington, D.C. They set fire to the White House, the U.S. Capitol Building, and many other government buildings.

Dolly Madison, President James Madison's wife, was forced to run from the White House in terror.

On September 12, 1814, British war ships sailed into Chesapeake Bay. The British wanted to capture the city of Baltimore. But first they had to get past Fort McHenry, which guarded the city. The people of Baltimore prepared for war—training, digging trenches, and tearing sheets for bandages. If the British took Baltimore, it would be a crushing blow for the United States.

On a tiny boat eight miles from Fort McHenry, a thirty-three-year-old lawyer named Francis Scott Key paced back and forth nervously. Key's friend, Dr. William Beanes, had been arrested by the British. Key had permission from President James Madison to gain Beanes' freedom.

Key sailed among the British warships, flying a white flag of peace. He boarded the ship where Beanes was held prisoner. In his hand, Key had a letter for the British commander. The letter was from British prisoners of war. In the letter, the British prisoners said that the Americans had treated them well.

The British commander said that one kindness deserved another. He said he would release Dr. Beanes. But the attack on Ft. McHenry and Baltimore was about to begin. Key and Beanes had to stay onboard the British warship. Soon, the two Americans had front-row seats watching the British attack on Baltimore.

At 7:00 a.m., September 13, the bombing began. All through the day Key could see a huge American flag flying above Ft. McHenry. He knew that as long as that flag flew, the British had not taken the fort. Sometimes the flag would disappear behind clouds of smoke. At night, the flag faded into the darkness.

All through the night, cannonballs bombed the fort. Rockets slashed across the sky. Red glares from the hot metal streaked into the fort. During the long, miserable night the Americans watched as Ft. McHenry took hit after hit. Only when dawn came did they see the American flag still flying above the fort. Then they knew that the British had lost the battle.

Key was so moved by what he saw that he wrote a few lines of poetry on the back of an envelope. "Oh say can you see, by the dawn's early light...The land of the free and the home of the brave."

Released at last, Key worked on the poem as he sailed ashore. The next morning he brought the finished work to a printer's shop. By afternoon, the poem, "The Defense of Fort McHenry," was being passed from hand-to-hand in Baltimore. Soon the entire country was singing Key's poem to the tune of an English drinking song. Key's song soon became known as the "Star-Spangled Banner." It was officially made the national anthem of the United States of America on March, 3, 1931.

O! say, can you see, by the dawn's early light,

The British bombed Ft. McHenry in Baltimore Maryland for 25 hours. The bombs fell from 7:00 a.m. September 13 to 8:00 a.m. September 14, 1814.

Now that the sun has risen, can you clearly see...

What so proudly we hailed at the twilight's last gleaming?

FRANCIS SCOTT KEY
1779-1843

The author of the "Star-Spangled Banner", Francis Scott Key, had dinner with the British commanders hours before they began the bombing. Key was asking for his friend's freedom from the British.

The flag that we saluted the night before as the sun went down.

Whose broad stripes and bright stars through the perilous fight,

The actual flag that flew at Fort McHenry. Notice the soldier beneath it.

The stripes of the flag were broad indeed. The flag that flew over Ft. McHenry had fifteen stars and stripes. It was huge— 42 feet long and 30 feet wide. The stars alone were 2 feet across. Today, the flag can still be seen at the Smithsonian Institution.

The flag's large stars and stripes could be seen through the dangerous battle.

*O'er the ramparts we watched were so gallantly
streaming,*

Even though the British rained bombs on Ft. McHenry for 25 hours, only four Americans were killed and twenty-four wounded. Many called it a miracle that so few were injured.

Over the fort we saw the flag flying in all its glory.

And the rocket's red glare, the bombs bursting in air,

The British fired over 1,500 cannonballs at Ft. McHenry. Each bomb weighed over 220 pounds.

The rockets and bombs lit up the sky...

Gave proof through the night that our flag was still there.

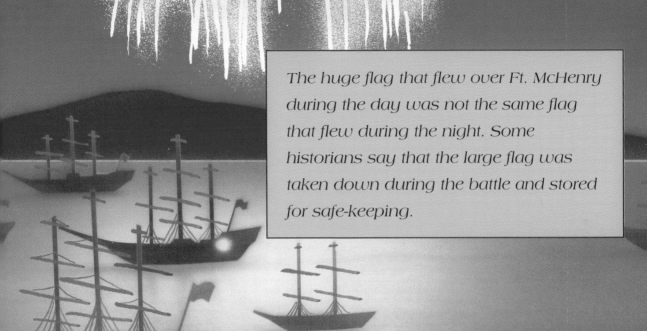

The huge flag that flew over Ft. McHenry during the day was not the same flag that flew during the night. Some historians say that the large flag was taken down during the battle and stored for safe-keeping.

The light from the rockets showed during the night that the flag was still flying.

O! say, does that Star-spangled Banner still wave

The flag that flew above Ft. McHenry weighed 200 pounds, cost $405.90, and used more than 400 yards of cloth. It was sewn by Mary Young Pickersgill.

Does that flag still fly...

O'er the land of the free and the home of the brave?

Because neither side gained or lost territory in the War of 1812, it was known at the time as "The War that Nobody Won."

Over the United States— the land of freedom.

FINAL WORD

Francis Scott Key finished the final verses to the "Star-Spangled Banner" in a hotel room in Baltimore. When he wrote the poem he had a special melody in mind— a song called "To Anacreon in Heaven." It was a song sung by a British social club. When Key published the poem he wrote on it "Tune: To Anacreon in Heaven." Anacreon was a Greek poet who lived from 572-488 B.C.

Key's song was an instant success, but soon faded away. It was revived by United States military bands in the 1890s. It did not become the official national anthem until an act of Congress made it so in 1931. Today, no professional baseball, football, basketball, or hockey game begins without the singing of "The Star-Spangled Banner".

THE STAR-SPANGLED BANNER

O! say, can you see, by the dawn's early light,
    What so proudly we hail at the twilight's last gleaming:
Whose broad stripes and bright stars through the perilous fight,
    O'er the ramparts we watched were so gallantly streaming,
And the rockets red glare, the bombs bursting in air,
Gave proof through the night that our flag was still there;

    O! say, does that Star-spangled Banner still wave
    O'er the land of the free and the home of the brave?

On the shore, dimly seen through the mists of the deep,
    Where the foe's haughty host in dread silence reposes,
What is that which the breeze, o'er the towering steep,
    As it fitfully blows, half conceals, half discloses?
Now it catches the gleam of the morning's first beam—
In full glory reflected, now shines on the stream;

    'Tis the Star-spangled Banner, O! long may it wave
    O'er the land of the free and the home of the brave.

And where is that band who so vauntingly swore
    That the havoc of war and the battle's confusion
A home and a country should leave us no more?
    Their blood has washed out their foul footsteps' pollution.
No refuge could save the hireling and slave.
From the terror of flight or the gloom of the grave!

    And the Star-spangled Banner in triumph doth wave
    O'er the land of the free and the home of the brave.

O! thus be it ever when free men shall stand
    Between their loved homes and the foe's destination;
Bless'd with victory and peace, may our Heaven-rescued land
    Praise the Power that hath made and preserved us a nation.
Then conquer we must, for our cause it is just—
    And this be our motto — "In God is our trust!"

    And the Star-spangled Banner in triumph shall wave
    O'er the land of the free and the home of the brave.

FRANCIS SCOTT KEY

GLOSSARY

Banner - a flag.

Broad - large or wide.

Gallantly - bravely.

Gleaming - shining.

Hailed - saluted.

National Anthem - an official song of praise about a nation.

O'er - over.

Perilous - dangerous.

Ramparts - the walls of a fort.

Spangled - bright and glittering.

Twilight - the last light of day before sunset.

DATE DUE

FOLLETT